THE GARDEN
WALL

THE LIBRARY *of* GARDEN DETAIL

THE GARDEN
WALL

MIRABEL OSLER

Simon and Schuster
New York   London   Toronto   Sydney   Tokyo   Singapore

Simon & Schuster
Simon & Schuster Building
Rockefeller Center
1230 Avenue of the Americas
New York, NY 10020

Text copyright © 1993 by Mirabel Osler
Photographic credits appear on page 63.

Designed by Paul Burgess
Printed in Singapore by Tien Wah

Library of Congress Cataloging-in-Publication Data

Osler, Mirabel.
  The garden wall/Mirabel Osler.
    p. cm—(The Library of garden detail)
  Includes bibliographical references.
  ISBN 0-671-79689-5
  1. Walls.   2. Wall gardens.   3. Garden structures.   I. Title.   II. Series.
TH4965.O83   1993
717—dc20

92-27716
CIP

10 9 8 7 6 5 4 3 2 1

CONTENTS

༺✦༻

6

*I*NTRODUCTION

*W*ALLS ARE THE SHEET ANCHOR OF GARDEN DESIGN. In centuries past, when labour and material were easily available, they provided a sense of magnificent grandeur to aristocratic mansions and stately homes. By dividing space with geometric precision they added grace or drama to manor houses and country estates. Courtyards, kitchen gardens, stabling and conservatories were enclosed by walls on a scale unthinkable today.

Even today, no garden should be without a wall – whether functional or frivolous. Think of gardens you have visited. Unless there is some kind of bony architecture constructed from wood, iron, stone or brick, a garden wilts. And of all a garden's elements, walls are the most powerful. Impracticable though our fleeting visions may be of making retreats like the paradise gardens of the Islamic world with

7

their walled sanctuaries, symbolic and sequestered, there are alternatives. Your garden may be small, but a place could surely be found for a curving dry-stone wall or a brick extension built at right-angles to the house. Basic and unadorned, inexpensive walls can form an integral part of a garden design today, even though the ideas for them might have generated from as remote a source as the courtyard gardens of Pompeii.

Walls seclude and they exclude; they can be used for shelter or for masking. A gardener living on a hill or on the coast – where ocean storms brutally shrivel plants with spray – is well aware of the benison provided by a wall. As long as it is carefully sited to minimize the effect of turbulence, it becomes an indispensable structure with its protective durability. And in a town, a kind of *enfilade* of right-angled jutting walls at regular intervals down the length of the garden allows for a variety of plants to satisfy their differing needs for sun, for shade or cosseting from frost. Less ambitiously, buttresses at regular intervals along a boundary wall add a sense of architectural solidity and a smudgy effect from charcoal shadows.

Hestercombe in Somerset, England, is an example of the idyllic symbiosis which unfailingly exists between walls

1. *A perfect example of how terracing and retaining walls can transform a slope. The lower wall grows naturally out of the land without any sense of contrivance.*

and plants. As it does, too, between retaining walls and slopes. Every slope can be improved by terracing, whether the retaining walls are used austerely, as in Wales, where leaden-grey striations of slates make a sombre background to hectic pink roses, or whether, as I have seen in California, a bank is decoratively retained by scalloped tiles forming 'fish scales' filled with dwarf campanulas. In both examples the slopes are lifted from the ordinary to the inspired.

2. I love this. The bleached mauve iris in the foreground, as pale as Lady's Smock, picks up the tone of the foxgloves and saves the reds from curdling.

Gertrude Jekyll, who is so encouraging about planting in walls, says: 'There is hardly any garden plant that does well in a flower border that will not do as well – in some cases much better – in a wall. . . .' Her advice is to sow seeds in the wall rather than putting in plants.

When you are making your choice, do not be daunted by size and think only of lewisias, *Erinus alpinus* and the ubiquitous house leek; be bold and go for foxgloves and mulleins – their spires look stately rising above the top of the wall. Wallflowers and valerian, which have a charming habit of wandering, are plants I long to lure to my walls; as far as I am concerned, however, there are no walls anywhere which deserve to be vandalized by *Cotoneaster horizontalis*. And beware of snow-in-summer. Do not be carried away by its cool name or a friend's generosity in dividing up plants; be ruthless and banish this pretty white-and-silver thug from ever appearing in your wall. Its life-style is far too errant.

Use small walls like an artist with a pencil. A low wall can work as an understatement – an eyebrow outlining a special feature – half enclosing the reflective eye of a pool or delineating a cluster of species tulips. In our garden, where we had a high bank above a curve in the stream, we made a 50 cm/18 inch wall about 4.75 m/14 ft long, without purpose except to create a pencil stroke emphasising the contour above the brook. The wall emerged from a *Viburnum opulus* 'Compactum' and vanished into 'Paul's Himalayan Musk', a white rose of prodigious splendour.

If materials, money, time or lack of expertise are not deterrents, a crinkum-crankum wall will provide both a fascinating and artistic form, and the different facets of its serpentine shape will provide wonderful planting possibilities. At Heveningham Hall in Suffolk, England, there is an imposing eighteenth-century example, originally designed for growing fruit. The same design could be adapted to support all manner of climbing plants. Madness might be invoked in a large garden by having a pair leading towards an important vista or object, like long wavy ribbons fairly close together. I can imagine tilting from side to side as one staggered in enchanted bemusement from a plethora of plants towards the distant glimpse of escape.

American gardeners have a particular flair when it comes to walls. They know when to stop. Where we are inclined to regard a wall as a vehicle for plants, in America I found their discretionary restraint between the use of

3 *An unusual way to cover a brick wall, giving a restful and textural appearance; it must need scrupulous maintenance. Without having the geometric outlines built into the brick, which show up so clearly, the wall would be unremarkable.*

structure and adornment, was an eye-opener. I saw in one small courtyard in San Francisco, the almost purpley-blue stones had been dressed with austerly cropped ivy in a diamond design. The wall was not there for practical support but for artistic decorum – not a vestige of floral expression was allowed to appear. On Long Island, the use of a wall and terrace of the same bricks, where the fold from vertical to horizontal was unembellished, made a geometric box for pots, one bench and a tree. The effect was aesthetic and spare. Another of their ideas which, if our summers in Britain continue to be hot we could copy, is their use of sheltering walls to extend the living area into the outside; a sitting or dining room becomes a roofless compartment unified with the house. There is great charm to this form of architecture where vines, clematis or fine bamboo stakes form a shadowy canopy overhead; in other outside rooms we sat in the open, but with a sense of protection and privacy from walls high enough to hide our surroundings except for a narrow squint either side.

4. *The view is enhanced by the dark walls festooned by a clematis. And the crimson camellia is made more dynamic by the pale furniture.*

14

Walls with apertures in them are perfection. Somehow, having a dominant sense of enclosure from the walls, and a bull's-eye window drawing you involuntarily to look through it to a view of kitchen garden, village roofs or countryside, is one of a garden's great seductions. At Hawkstone Park in Shropshire, England, there is a 'grotto' in the precipitous cliffs, with a view through the circular opening onto the river far below. If your garden window is surrounded by roses or honeysuckle you have the double sensory indulgence from both vision and scent. The opening need not be round; it could be rectangular. But whether the rectangle of 'divine proportions' – what the ancient Greeks called the 'Golden Mean' (a ratio of 5:3) – is vertical or horizontal, that consummate mathematical correlation will draw you inexorably to see what lies beyond.

Bee boles were a traditional feature of walls that today can inspire a variety of schemes. Built as niches, in which one or two bee skeps were housed, they protected the hives from the weather. The recesses were often constructed in groups of six or more, though at Thornbury Castle in Avon, England, there were once as many as twenty-six. But for the gardener who is not into bees, cavities could be built into a new wall to make alcoves in which to grow plants, to place sculpture or pots, or for a grand display of theatrical splendour by using a light in every recess. More modestly, a row of small cavities, like the ones they have in Thai temples to hold candles, would be feasible for those of us who do not have a clue about constructional dynamics.

16

Without doubt, walls used for training fruit trees provide some of the most sublime garden ingredients there are. What need then of decoration or nooks, of canny planting or pretty pictures? Fan-trained morellos; espaliered apples and plums; bush, pyramid and cordon-pruned trees give such an architectural sense of pleasure that, whatever the season, their serene composure makes a garden complete. Even in winter, when the bare branches are spread out neat as fish bones, you have no need to be wishing it was some other month.

5. *Single, or as a series, the bee bole design can be built into a new wall.
Whether vacant, dark and curious, or used for ornament, lamp or plant,
the shape is good enough to be taken seriously.*

You need cement and foundations for the sophisticated brick walls like those still seen in kitchen gardens, but dry stone walls can be used almost anywhere. If you have the energy and the stone, even an aspiring garden bodger can

6. *The blackness of the stone, the colour of the lichen and the fallen leaves show up the beauty of an unembellished wall.*

hardly go wrong by constructing one of these. I dote on making walls – not tall ones, because I know they would collapse, but squat ones stout enough for pots to stand on and be shuffled round according to colour and height. Of course a well-constructed dry stone wall is another matter. If you had, say, a 1.50 m/4½ ft high wall made by a craftsman with the use of a batter frame (a tapering wooden frame to ensure the wall tapers slightly), with 'through-stones' tying the sides together and thin copestones standing upright along the top, then everything else in your garden would appear to go into orbit as you placed a specimen tree, a bench or fountain in relation to it. Peacocks in the foreground would not look bad either.

Here are some less highfalutin' ideas:

Fat stone walls, low enough to sit on and creating a different level from lawn and flowerbed, fit well along a terrace. If you build a wall that is damp and shady, leathery hart's-tongue and rusty-back ferns have a way of appearing with a seemingly artless sense of place. They do sometimes fool you: in a dry summer the ferns vanish to dust so that you sigh at their departure, only to be enchanted by their revival after the first rain.

Other walls, built with pockets of earth between the stones, can be stuffed with plants, looking like hundreds-and-thousands in a medley of colours; or, if you use only variations of one colour in your planting, you will achieve a quieter, more subtle effect from the tones of the flowers against the texture of the wall. Brick walls, though not as accommodating as stone, can also have plants growing from their earth-filled joints.

A trough of low brick walling filled with earth, its walls two bricks thick, will form raised beds for elderly or disabled gardeners, at a convenient height and close to the house. But keep your wits about you when choosing colours. Some bricks are such a raucous red that, when planted with a filling of purple or yellow pansies, the visible decibels are increased to a pitch of environmental disaster.

Flat-backed ceramic pots hanging on walls, when filled with flowers well chosen to harmonize with their background material, can look quite dashing. But, unlike pots on the ground, they require a steadfast watering commitment.

7. *A fine example of the use of small niches in a wall; this could easily be copied when building a new wall.*

For really spirited inspiration on how to design, build and clothe brick walls, visit Stone House Cottage Nurseries in Worcestershire, England. There James Arbuthnott has built (is still building) towers, alcoves, cloisters and

8. One of James Arbuthnott's constructions growing out of the angle of the walls, with windows onto the countryside.

embrasures, as well as walls, against which he and his wife, Louisa, grow every kind of docile or way-out plant which thrives on the guardianship of Kidderminster brick.

People who live among flint are blessed. What marvellous walls these knapped stones make, set in regular squares outlined in limestone or brick, with their white rind and oystery facets catching the light. They are so beautiful you need to be forbearing: too many plants and all is concealed.

If you can contrive it, have recycled water trickling from two or three small, shell-shaped basins growing out of a wall. Visually pretty, the lulling sound is balm to the ears on a sweltering summer's day.

White walls made of rubblestone or breeze blocks and plastered over make dazzling backgrounds for plumbago or bignonia in more southern countries. But why not elsewhere? The render could be painted apricot, tobacco or lavender-grey as a more suitably-coloured foil for a whole spectrum of climbing plants. If you used brick with a light membrane of plaster, the trendy 'distressed look' could easily be achieved, with bricks squinting through the decrepitude.

The tops of walls can be elaborated in all sorts of imaginative ways: by achieving ornamental symmetry with finials, pineapples, balls or obelisks; by a rhythmical pattern of crenellations; or by a notched pediment. In areas where thatching is still a tradition, using it along the top of a brick or cobbled wall gives a bucolic and textural effect which

*9. Curved bricks make a pleasing open pattern
for the top of this wall, though the stone
pediments seem too oppressive for the structure to
be entirely successful.*

needs little in the way of floral adornment. Whatever you use, be parsimonious when it comes to planting; think carefully when choosing plants to clothe your wall. Ivy and Russian vine are predators, while climbing and rambler

24

roses appropriate walls with voracity, and once established only the most stony-hearted could bear to decapitate them.

Nor need walls be solid. For wildly beautiful inspiration turn to Moorish and Mughal architecture. Such immoderate effects may at first sight seem outlandishly out of kilter with our western gardens, but what lacy delights could be adapted from those ornamental fenestrations, in patterns varying from hexagons to yin and yang. Or, more prosaically but equally effectively, make a *clair-voyée* like the very early eighteenth-century one at Westbury Court in Gloucestershire, where you want to make a boundary less emphatic than a wall; by using iron balustrading mounted at intervals on a low wall between piers of brick or stonework, you would lead the eye beyond the garden, and would create a handsome and more substantial effect than by the use of trellis. But one final warning! However pressed you are, never, never think you can get away with those openwork concrete lengths sold in DIY stores.

If you can pull it off, a fake ruined wall can work

25

wonderfully when glimpsed distantly through greenery. If
you fail, you are left with an eyesore.

Doors! In walls they are irresistible. Closed, they
provoke a sort of nosy speculation; ajar, they work like a
beckoning finger. Seats built into walls have great charm. At
Broughton Castle in Oxfordshire there is a seat so
integrated that you can almost sense the warmth from the
stonemason's hands as he eased the seat into the curve of
the wall.

In France I have seen Delft tiles set into a plastered
wall; in Italy majolica tiles are used to face the walls of
cloisters, and in Spain flowers and birds extravagantly
painted on tiles, their background white almost blue, form a
showy setting for a variety of flower pots.

Carefully cut turf sandwiched between stones, rubble,
bricks, cobbles, or a mixture of whatever is available, make
rustic walls. Sown with seeds the fids of earth will flower, so
in time you have a homogeneous wall which serenely fits
into garden wilderness.

Here is some useful advice given to me by an experienced wall designer and builder. Trivial as they seem,

10. *A doorway in a wall seldom fails. This one is cleverly left half unadorned so that the outline of the opening makes a geometric frame to what lies beyond. The subdued colour of the santolinas in the foreground match the patina of the wall.*

these points are seldom written about yet are so intrinsic that they can change something merely functional into something felicitous. First, when choosing materials *look at what surrounds you*. Use local material. Secondly, a wall should appear to grow out of the ground – not balance on it. Therefore you must dig out a little trough for the foundation layer of stone to lie in – even if you half hide the first line do not grudge the waste. (For a brick wall you will, of course, need proper foundations.) Thirdly, if you give the capping of a wall a slight overhang like that on a pediment or window sill, it will create a dark underline of shadow which, even if you are not aware how it works, will give the wall a sense of perfect coordination. Finally, never underestimate mortar. Use sharp sand, not builders' sand, with grains up to .6 cm/¼ inch; a good mix is three parts sand, one of lime and half of cement.

After that advice I shall never build a wall again. But here in this book are what other people have done. Imaginative or resourceful, prosaic or bizarre – whatever these photographs inspire in you, they do show how a wall clasps a garden.

28

ℐMPOSING
𝒲ALLS

11. *A very powerful curved and crenellated wall, with steps at one side,
which might have appeared to overwhelm the rows of standard roses
edged with lavender, but for the width of the grassy path in the foreground.*

30

12. *The fairly austere effect from wall and greenery do not distract from the important urn. Even the wisteria appears unobtrusive, flowing away from the focal point and down the descending levels of the stonework.*

13 & 14. *These two crinkle-crankle walls have been treated very differently. One has been left unadorned, so that the perspective from the diminishing curves stands out clearly in contrast to the straight path running alongside. The other is lushly planted at ground level, creating shadowy bits from the contours of the wall.*

31

15. *What a nice design for a city garden wall. The 'blind' arches make it much more interesting, and the foliage around the lion's head and water trough give an asymmetrical air to the overall appearance.*

16. *Flanked by yew trees, the niche and statue have weathered over the years. The wall is greatly enhanced by the patterns of lichen and the small ferns and grasses which have been left to grow along the top.*

17. *I like the look of the bricks squinting through the render of a wall draped with* Wisteria sinensis *and* W. floribunda, *rising out of* Abutilon vitifolium, Olearia gunniana *and a yellow* Azara serrata.

34

18. *You almost feel the wall had to be built especially tall so that it could support this quite dramatic ceanothus,* C. dentatus. *What on earth would you do with this species if you didn't have such a wall?*

19. Basking lemons in terracotta pots the colour of the background must thrive in the reflected heat from the wall. I'm not sure the balustrade below does anything for this composition.

36

20. *The buttressed wall integrates beautifully with the buildings behind and the use of trellis, the colour of the stone, allows for a* Clematis tangutica *to ramp up and over the top.*

RURAL WALLS

21. *Alpine plants, which do better sown as seed rather than planted, growing in a dry-stone wall with plenty of space for soil.*

38

22. *A superb dry-stone wall in a Lutyens/Jekyll garden of great fame.*
The bold combination of diminishing steps and the walls either side,
combined with arbitrary flowers, show to perfection how plants and static
structures have a natural empathy.

23. *An old farmhouse dry-stone wall appropriated by ferns will, later in the year, be covered in roses. The foldyard has been excavated to make a pond surrounded by kingcups, primulas, iris and mimulas.*

39

24. *Another dry-stone wall showing how attractive the worked coping stones look when laid on their edges.*

40

25. *An orchard like this, protected by high brick walls, is beyond most of us. But even so, given the space, a modest enclosure might be feasible, built out from the existing walls of house, garage or barn.*

26. *An espalier fruit tree, fastidiously pruned, decorates the wall with mathematical precision and makes a contrasting background for the flowery profusion of a herbaceous border.*

27. *A door left ajar in a high wall is tantalizing. And here the textured neutrality from wall, door and blossom create a restful combination which could be copied on a smaller scale, using oak, stone and a white flowering tree.*

43

28. *An effect any gardener would die for! Narrow terraces formed by stone retaining walls is one of the great gardening masterpieces. Ideas for what you plant there can gestate slowly, with relishing anticipation, knowing there is no urgency to clothe such walls.*

44

29 & 30. *These two photographs are examples of cottage flowers growing so favourably against walls. The combination works perfectly. A small wall can, without much expense, integrate with ease into a flower bed.*

31. *The cottage, the wall, the hydrangea and hollyhocks have a timeless appearance evoking all our ideas about how English villages should look.*

32. *A* clair-voyée *such as this could easily be incorporated into a wall you are building – whatever the material. I suppose the plain wall top provoked the owner to put the lamp up there.*

46

GLIMPSES

THROUGH

33. *The render on this brick wall surrounding a city garden is peeling away in places to give a well-worn effect of starkness in contrast to the ebulliant* Rosa banksiae lutea.

48

34. *The wall is almost invisible behind the copious rose, 'Bantry Bay', on the left of the doorway. The dilemma for the gardener with a wall is to know when to indulge in climbing plants and when to be temperate. Here the prodigality is in perfect contrast with the uncluttered lawn beyond.*

35. *A wall topped by tiles gives a very un-English look to the
enclosure, and the glimpse of a garden beyond this informally planted
pool is intriguing.*

50

36. *A circular window in a wall can make a focal point. Here the opening is filled with greenery, which gives an entirely different look from the next picture.*

37. *An example of architecture, perspective and garden design highlighted by deliberately looking at the garden as though through a lens. In the garden there are several other types of openings in walls.*

38. *These old brick walls, built so closely parallel to each other, create an unusual effect with narrowing lines leading to a doorway at the far end.*

ᗪECORATIVE ᗯALLS

39. *An Italian wall to inspire a gardener to be adventurous. The weathering may have taken centuries to acquire, but the design and colour might be adapted for a small enclosing wall near the house.*

40 & 41. *Containers fixed to a wall are a good idea when they are carefully sited and the colours chosen to harmonize with the background material. Arbitrarily dotted on a large wall they lack cohesion and the plan falls to pieces.*

54

42. *Three small stone shapes, like cupped hands, have been built out of the wall where water trickles out of sticks of hollow elder. The moss, ferns and perpetual moisture have a smell of sappy dankness.*

43. *Like a sentry box with a plain wooden seat, James Arbuthnott has incorporated the shelter into his wall as a small perching place for contemplating the garden.*

44. *The fiercely flamboyant colours, framed within a stone arch, are set against the distant view of massive summer foliage – restful and serene.*

45. *The last four photographs are delightfully bizarre. Here the door
built into such an outlandish wall, full of fluttering plants, looks as
though it leads to the land of hobgoblins.*

46. *The homogeneous appearance of this collection of different materials, make a wall of great style and humour, held together by a traditional notched pediment.*

60

47. *First break your crockery. It would be worth it to make a wall like this one, flippancy doesn't often appear in gardens.*

48. *I kept this for the last. An inspired background 'wall' made from glass bottles and an occasional shell, where the terracotta bust, demoted to ground level, contemplates more bottles flowing away from under him.*

S O U R C E S

Some UK Addresses

Conservation Building Products
Forge Works
Forge Lane
Cradley Heath
Warley
West Midlands
Telephone: 0384 69551

Some US Addresses

M&A Landscape Service
193 Birch Hill Road
Locust Valley, NY 11560
Telephone: (516) 676-0980

Walpole Woodworkers
767 East Street
Walpole, MA 02081
Telephone: (508) 668-2800

Stewart Ironworks Co.
P.O. Box 2612
Covington, KY 41012
Telephone: (606) 431-1985

Boren Clay Products
P.O. Box 368
Pleasant Garden, NC 27313
Telephone: (919) 674-2255

Dunis Studios
HC 53, Box 3125
Bulverde, TX 78163
Telephone: (512) 438-7715

Contact your local chamber
of commerce for other
sources in your area.

PICTURE CREDITS

The publisher thanks the following photographers and
organizations for their kind permission to reproduce photographs
in this book.
Owners and designers of gardens are credited where known.
Photographers appear in bold type.

Title page: **Derek Fell**; Stonecrop, Hudson Valley, NY, USA
page 6 **Hugh Palmer**; Balcaskie House
Picture No 1 **Jerry Harpur**; Wadhurst Park, West Sussex
Picture No 2 **Derek Fell**; Old Westbury Garden, NY, USA
Picture No 3 **Derek Fell**; New Orleans, Louisianna, USA
Picture No 4 **Jerry Harpur**; Viscountess Stuart of Findhorn (designer)
private garden, London
Picture No 5 **Hugh Palmer**; Horam Hall
Picture No 6 **Derek Fell** Cedaridge Farm, Bucks County, PA, USA
Picture No 7 **Andrew Lawson**; Edzell Castle, Scotland
Picture No 8 **Jerry Harpur**; James Arbuthnott (designer) Stone House Cottage,
Hereford & Worcestershire
Picture No 9 **Derek Fell**; Dumbarton Oaks, Washington DC, USA
Picture No 10 **Andrew Lawson**; Broughton Castle, Oxfordshire
Picture No 11 **Jerry Harpur;** Hazelbury Manor, Wiltshire
Picture No 12 **Derek Fell**; Dumbarton Oaks, Washington DC, USA
Picture No 13 **Derek Fell**; Richmond, Virginia, USA
Picture No 14 **Jerry Harpur**; Paul Miles (designer)
Picture No 15 **Derek Fell**; Charleston, SC, USA
Picture No 16 **Hugh Palmer**; Garsington Manor
Picture No 17 **Andrew Lawson**; Univercity Botanic Garden, Oxford
Picture No 18 **Andrew Lawson**; University Botanic Garden, Oxford
Picture No 19 **Derek Fell**; Filoli Garden, CA, USA
Picture No 20 **Hugh Palmer**; Abbotswood, Gloucestershire
Picture No 21 **Derek Fell**; Stonecrop, Hudson Valley, NY, USA
Picture No 22 **Jerry Harpur**; Hestercombe House, Somerset

63

64